The Obvious Secret Lesson of the Wizard of Oz

A Metaphysical Interpretation

By Helen Gordon

**The Obvious Secret Lessons of the Wizard of Oz,
A Metaphysical Interpretation
Helen Gordon.**

First Edition

June 2012

ISBN 978-0615607504

Cover Design by Clearly Written

Table of Contents

Acknowledgment

Thank you David Boufford (Mr. Positive.com) for encouraging me to write this book and having the insight of its value. You are truly a spiritually gifted business coach.

Rodney Bleam, I thank God for you. Jayne Whittaker, thank you for the downtime reminders. Rev. Daytra Hansel, your encouragement and dynamic prayers are such a blessing. Elvira Bohle, your inspiration continues to uplift and keep me moving forward. Maria Hauser-Sauper, your energy touches my soul.

Introduction

Each of the characters in the Wizard of Oz story will be identified in your life. No longer will the wicked witches (male or female) of your life be able to affect your emotions. You can strongly reclaim your power and emotional control as you begin to accept the support of your spiritual red slippers.

This book does not lead you to outside sources for emotional healing; it guides you to using your own mind, thoughts and power. All you need is within you.

For those who are struggling to understand *"A Course In Miracles,"* especially about reality, this book simplifies those principles. A novice will grasp the principles more clearly; the experienced will learn more; teachers will gain a new tool;

and all will deepen their spiritual understanding.

Additionally, this book provides more clarity and understanding of general metaphysical concepts. All of this "inner power" stuff will make more sense.

Terminology

Although Christian terminology is found in this book, it is different from its traditional usage:

- The **ego** is that loud inner critic. Wrong-thinking. Offers unfavorable choices.

- The **Course** is "A Course In Miracles" text.

- **Forgiveness** is not a pardon, but a correction in perception and the freedom to move on.

- The **Holy Spirit** is your inner Voice, divine Guide, and spiritual Being. That part of you which is always in communication with God. It is who you truly are, the voice for God.

- **Illusions** are your daily human being experiences. It seems that most folks who have had a brush with death do not find these experiences to be as important.

- **Self**, in upper case, your true Being that guides you rightly, is always in connection and agreement with God. It is not physical.

- **self**, in lowercase, refers to the human personality that is influenced by the ego. It is physical.

- **Voice** is your inner guide for right choices, your holy Spirit's voice.

Dorothy

1

Dorothy

"We often have dark moments when things seem threatening and terrifying. On our journey, we may encounter darkness with no apparent way around it. Sometimes it is through the seeming darkness that we reach our goal."

– Helen Gordon

D orothy (Can't you see my pain?)

The Wizard of Oz, a 100-year old story, reveals the significance and support of relationships in our lives. It also simplifies many of the principles of *A Course In Miracles* (the Course), a teaching of judgment, enemies, love and forgiveness.

Author Lyman Frank Baum (1856-1919), simplifies a complicated concept of gratitude and forgiveness by turning it into an entertaining fairytale, starring the orphan, Dorothy Gale.

In the beginning of the 1939 Metro Goldwyn Mayer (MGM) movie version of the Wizard of Oz story, Dorothy was frantic that her dog, Toto, would be taken away or harmed as a result of his behavior. Toto chased Miss Almira Gulch's cat and trampled her flowers whenever they passed her house. Dorothy urged his innocence and found excuses for him in spite of his destructive behavior.

Miss Gulch, of little patience, threatened Dorothy and Toto each time they passed by her house. In Dorothy's mind, she had a monumental problem with Miss Gulch and no one cared to help her resolve it; everyone seemed oblivious to her pain; no one seemed to have interest in hearing about her conflict.

Desperately, she wanted someone, anyone, to agree that her choice was not misconduct. In Dorothy's mind, her innocence was being ignored by everyone. She thought that change needed to come from Miss Gulch (projection of guilt), not her.

Hunk, one of the workers at her Uncle's farm, offered a good simple solution to her conflict, "Don't go past Miss Gulch's house!"[1]

Here was a very simple solution to Dorothy's problem, the power to create a peaceful relationship with Miss Gulch. Dorothy was blind to her contribution to the problem. She had been warned many times of Toto's unacceptable behavior and its unpleasant consequences, but insisted on exercising her "right" to walk past Miss Gulch's house.

How much trouble would it have been for her peace of mind, as well as for Miss Gulch, to choose another route? Dorothy could have chosen to allow peace instead of chaos between them. Too often, the ego convinces us to choose the defiant path to prove a useless point.

Miss Gulch obtained a court order to take Toto away from Dorothy. Training Toto could have mended the relationship. However, she considered herself the victim to a mean and cruel person whom she referred to as a wicked witch.

The love of her life, what she valued most, was taken away. Just when she thought this love was gone forever, Toto escaped the clutches of Miss Gulch and returned to the farm.

Rather than change her route (change her mind), Dorothy scooped up Toto and ran away from home to escape the dreadful problem no one seemed to care about, which was the threat of separation from her dear Toto (source of love) and only friend.

Some of us run away literally, while others run to drugs, alcohol, or some other temporary conscious escape from what seems to be a hopeless unloving situation or separation from love. We avoid taking responsibility for creating the absence of the love we desire.

On her journey to nowhere, Dorothy met Professor Marvel, a traveling magician. He pretended to read her future, using a crystal ball, and provided a false prediction of Aunt Em's illness to purposely frighten Dorothy to return home.

The magician appealed to her emotion (ego) and guilt to influence her return home. It worked, for she frantically headed back home with Toto in tow.

The journey back home was a frightening one for Dorothy as a storm approached. Nothing was stable; nothing seemed safe; it was quickly growing unusually dark. Horrified, she ended up facing an enormous tornado, and then life got out of control in a very big way. The sky grew even darker.

Dorothy ran for safety, pulled at the storm door, but it would not open. No one could hear her cries for help. Desperately, she ran inside the house and rushed through her bedroom door where an object struck her head, rendering her unconscious.

Symbolically, in this unconscious state of mind, Dorothy had lost her way home, separated from the family she loved, and entered a dream state as the house spun violently in the eye of the tornado (confused and overwhelmed by life's challenges).

Now, the Course says that we have merely fallen asleep and only need to awaken from the dream. In Dorothy's dream, she found herself in an imaginary world of Oz. This becomes her new reality and world of victimization. The obvious secret lesson begins.

Her new life of victimization first began in Munchkin Land, where her spinning house fatally landed on the Wicked Witch of the East. In appreciation of this fatality, which ended wicked control, Dorothy mysteriously found herself instantly wearing the dead witch's ruby red slippers.

Although killing the wicked witch ended evil in Munchkin Land, Dorothy's guilt marched forward for murdering the witch.

Guilt is how the ego drastically discounted her success at ending evil. She held on to this guilt in spite of having brought peace and joy to the land. The Course says that guilt seeks punishment and finds it. And plenty of it comes her way throughout her journey.

Glinda, the good witch of the North, appeared and explained the value of Dorothy's red slippers. From a metaphysical perspective, these slippers represented her intuitive guidance, protection, and power over all things, obstacles, and situations. She could surely find her way back home, having all she needed.

All Dorothy wanted at this point was to get back to Kansas (home) and so began the whole story of her journey back home. She had wanted to leave her unkind conditions in Kansas so badly, but after achieving it, all she could think about was returning home.

Before Dorothy set off on her journey home, Glinda warned her, "Never ever take those ruby slippers off your feet for a moment or you are at the mercy of the Wicked Witch of the West."[2] It is similar to *remembering* our power, not losing sight of it, or trying to give it away, lest we fall under the influence of the ego.

To remain on course (the right path of our goal) we must call upon this power that walks beside us wherever we go and is available at any point of our life's journey.

The good witch, Glinda, sent Dorothy off to Emerald City to find the Wizard of Oz, who would have the directions for her way back home.

"How do I start to Emerald City?"[3] Dorothy asked.

"It's always best to start at the beginning,"[4] said Glinda.

The beginning was right where Dorothy stood. She simply had to get started on the path of her dreams, the yellow brick road, and then follow it.

Getting started can be a challenge when we are paralyzed by fear or indecisiveness (another form of fear). How ever small, how ever weak our belief, we must take action to obtain our desires. A mere start, regardless of momentum, is what will eventually help us reach a goal.

The yellow brick road can symbolize the right guidance of the Holy Spirit. It will lead us where we want to go if we but follow it. As a brick road, it becomes a physical form to help us remain focused and to stay on course.

On the road to Truth, we learn many lessons, create many new relationships, and conquer many challenges. Travels along the yellow brick road reveal strengths we did not know we had and allow us to use the ones we doubted.

Contrary, we find weaknesses we did not know we had. If we allow, our surprise information about our strengths and weaknesses become tools we can use to make good choices. We can use the power of our strengths to eliminate the limitations our weaknesses create. Within us is the intelligence to do this.

Characters in the movie went seeking outside themselves for things considered critical to feeling complete. They felt incomplete, that somehow they were lacking in some area. These things became their *issues;* life would have no joy without these things.

The Course says we lack nothing. We have all we need, right within us. What we want is merely being denied. Denial dictates we seek gurus, rituals and things to help us get rid of our lack. When these things fail, they are declared the cause of our alleged lack and are used to validate our claim to our reality and power of our issues. Failure can only *seem* to have happened because there is no lack to remove.

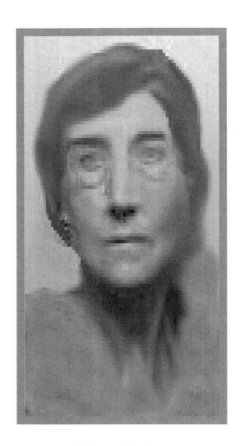

Miss Gulch

Miss Gulch

"Under the disguise of "creativity" and "thinking outside the box", we break the rules for a false sense of freedom." – Helen Gordon

Miss Gulch (structure)

Ms. Gulch followed the straight and narrow path. Breaking rules was not tolerable, especially if it disrupted her life.

As with Toto, there are rules we want to break on our journey, even at cost. We want to do things our way and resist structure as if structure could harm us.

Under the disguise of *creativity* and *thinking outside the box*, we break the rules.

The temptation of defying structure is inviting, presenting a brief sense of freedom; however, it is a false sense of freedom. In that defiance, we wander off the path, meet with opposition and get ourselves in trouble. Defiance does not create our freedom; it already exists.

Convincingly, the ego claims that structure would rob us of our freedom; therefore, we would surely lose control of our lives. This is a false sense of control since we determine the control of our lives. Structure puts us in control, which decreases distractions and helps us stay on the path to that which we desire.

Defiance is a useless act which sabotages our ability and opportunity to receive what we are seeking. The energy it requires can detour our thoughts toward something meaningless.

What is meaningless is allowed to gain value. Once meaningless things are given value, they multiply and spread like a virus. This compounds the problem created by defiance.

Darkness obscures the path of our journey. Relinquishing the acts of defiance will bring back the light to illumine the way to our goal. Wicked witches become powerless again.

Scarecrow

3

The Scarecrow

"Often we are afraid to do something we desire for fear of failure. Usually, there is nothing to lose and the only sure way to success is a try." – Helen Gordon

S<u>carecrow</u> **(hung up)**

Scarecrow believed, "I am a failure because I have no brain."[5] He declared he was a victim, bullied by the crows. Victimization was his excuse for ignorance. This was an attempt to project his failure onto the crows through blame. Blame was used to prove that his stupidity and failure in his job to protect the crop were not his fault.

The crows were deemed proof of his alleged failure, uselessness and hopelessness in his career.

With very little self-confidence, Scarecrow asked Dorothy, "Do you think the Wizard will give me a brain?"[6] She responded, "I don't know, but even if he didn't, you wouldn't be worse off."[7]

Often we are afraid to do something we desire for fear of failure. Usually, there is nothing to lose and the only sure way to success is a try.

On the other hand, was Scarecrow's inquiry questioning his worthiness? This should never be an issue. As the Course says, "It is that you ask for far too little." [8] Our worth was established by God. We only need to accept God's high value of us.

Scarecrow joins Dorothy to obtain the brain (intelligence) he desired. At that moment, all possibilities of achieving his desires became available to him.

The common goal for Dorothy and Scarecrow was to meet the Wizard and to be granted their specific desires. Two had now joined for this common goal. Reaching the goal gained more certainty with this union.

Scarecrow was the incarnation of the worker, Hunk, on the Kansas farm. Hunk had the logical solution to Dorothy's conflict with Miss Gulch.

"Hunk: "Now look it, Dorothy. You ain't usin' your head about Miss Gulch. Think you didn't have any brains at all!"[9]

Dorothy: "I have so got brains."[10]

Hunk: "Well, why don't you use 'em? When you come home, don't go by Miss

Gulch's place. Then Toto won't get in her garden, and you won't get in no trouble, see?"[11]

Dorothy: "Oh, Hunk. You just won't listen, that's all."[12]

But who was the one not listening? A simple solution to end the conflict for Dorothy was presented to her but ignored. Her goal did not seem to be one to sincerely end her conflict, but to prove her victimhood.

Hunk was clear about the effectiveness of his solution. It is not always easy for our audience to accept our help. Therefore, we must move on or face the possibility of becoming stuck with them.

Blame is used to explain the reason for the failure at a task. "If it had not been for… I could have been successful I could be further along."

This is a common excuse for failure. The ego thinks that if it finds someone or something to blame, it will be granted pardon.

Failure is assigned a role of judgment against us. Fear kicks in and we begin our battle to prove our innocence by using blame to support our case.

Fortunately, there is no judgment; there is no case to prove; there is only a human experience customized by our choices.

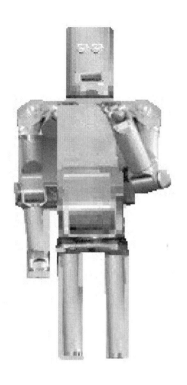

Tin Man

4

The Tin Man

"How often do we want to cry out for someone to help us, but have difficulty expressing it?"

– Helen Gordon

T in Man (stuck in the same place, stagnant)

Further along the yellow brick road, Dorothy and Scarecrow encounter a muffled cry for help. How often do we want to cry out for someone to help us, but have difficulty expressing it? We clam up for so long, that it becomes difficult to speak. It becomes a challenge to get the words out on our own.

Speaking up for ourselves becomes forbidden. Speaking out for something confronts us as an unfulfilled obligation. Oral expression is threatened by anticipated ridicule.

Our health benefits from speaking because when we express emotions, it allows us to release anxiety. It also allows us to release toxic thoughts, blocks and stress.

After listening intently they both realized that the Tin Man had rusted and could not move his mouth to speak. In fact, his whole body was rusted into its position. The thing Tin Man needed most to gain his freedom, an oil can, was just inches away from his grasp. (How close are we to our burning desires?)

Dorothy grabbed the oil can and lubricated Tin Man's joints, which gave him free movement and freedom to speak. Tin

Man felt so good about it he danced.

We sometimes become stuck in our old thinking, in a box, with no flexibility to do things differently. Contentment with the old ways of doing things can possibly alienate us from others. If others are not interested in our outdated opinions or ideas, emotional separation happens and we become defensive outcasts.

Tin Man felt that, "If only I had a heart, then...." He had the "If only" blues. Oh how much he could do; oh what he could be "if only......" He was depressed, deep in self-pity, paralyzed by his belief that what he had was not enough. These are also emotions that can devastate the heart, creating a host of stress-related diseases.

Tin Man was the incarnation of the worker, Hickory, on the Kansas farm. He was working on a metal object when interrupted by the commotion of Dorothy falling into the pig sty.

Here we have the brainless Scarecrow who *thought* about going to the Wizard and the emotionless Tin Man who was *depressed*, both claiming they did not have what they sought from the Wizard.

Each was so much into their own victimization and shortcomings that they did not even see the truth about each other. So off they all went to see the Wizard.

Dorothy, Scarecrow, and Tin Man merrily skipped down the yellow brick road where they inevitably had to pass through a dark and creepy forest (darkness in life) they did not like. It was frightening. Surely something wicked lurked in the darkness waiting to harm them.

dark night of the soul

We often have dark moments, moments when things seem threatening and terrifying. On our journey, we may encounter darkness with no apparent way around it. <u>Sometimes it is through the seeming darkness that we safely reach our goal.</u>

As they walked through the darkness, Scarecrow said, "It will get darker before lighter."

However, nothing on that dark and creepy portion of the journey would have or could have hurt them. Couldn't have told them that at one point when the ferocious Lion leaped out to block their path.

We know what horrible things a Lion can do! After all, he is the king of the jungle! It says so in the encyclopedia (it is a fact?). *deo* <u>Lions are not friendly and are known to devour intruders we are told.</u> hmmm?

30

Lion

5

The Lion

"We do not have to accept anyone's opinion of us. It is only an opinion that cannot change who we really are."
– Helen Gordon

L**ion (terrified boaster, bully)**

Just like the ego, Lion was just an all-talk bully. He boasted and growled, trying to frighten everyone, hiding behind his façade of bravery. People can appear fearless when hiding their cowardice with boasts, aggression, intimidation, and put-downs.

If you know any lions in your life, face them. These lions can be people, places or activities. Whatever has you too fearful to move forward, that something has your life on hold and can be pushed aside with your own strength and courage.

Lion confronted Dorothy, Scarecrow and Tin Man, got in their face, and then verbally put down each one harshly. He needed to destroy their belief in themselves to make himself look more powerful. This verbal abuse toward his victims was what he really believed to be true about himself.

Wow!

(Narsisstic behavior) -

At first, Scarecrow, Tin Man and Dorothy shivered in terror by his words and accepted what he said to be truth. They believed they were those awful things he claimed. However, it was only an opinion; moreover, it was an opinion of a coward.

We do not have to accept anyone's opinion of us. It is only an opinion; it cannot change who we truly are. We cannot allow someone's opinion to be real for us.

Inspirational speaker, Les Brown, was once told, "Someone's opinion of you does not have to become your reality."

Bro. Ishmael Tetteh says, "How can you allow your life to be run by opinions of people who themselves do not know why they have those opinions?"

Lion turned to Toto in a position of attack. At that moment, Dorothy suddenly found courage in spite of her fear and stood up to Lion! Something she valued very much was threatened so she fought back fearlessly to protect it.

Dorothy let go of her fears for an instant to face the dangerous challenge! Lion backed down without a fight. True courage had revealed itself and nothing could successfully oppose it. (Love) found the hidden courage and pushed fear aside.

We too only need to find courage to stand up against those challenges that seem surely to beat us, consume us, or kill us. A little courage is necessary for us to move things out of the way and get on with our journey.

Remember, we are always wearing those powerful ruby slippers, determined to find our way back home. The Holy Spirit is always guiding us when we allow ourselves to follow the safe yellow brick road.

Sometimes we question our worthiness of this guidance. Lion questioned his worthiness to join the trio when they invited him to come along to find courage for himself. He responded, "Wouldn't you feel degraded to be seen in the company of a cowardly lion?"[13]

This is comparison and sign of low self-esteem. It is the not-good-enough song we may hear humming in our ears from time to time. Some of us accuse others of not respecting our worth, when it is really our own judgment about ourselves. As a result, we attract that which validates our beliefs. The ego is determined to be right.

Being king of the jungle, there were expectations of a lion's behavior described in his encyclopedia that Lion knew he would not be able to fulfill.

An animal research expert of sorts had defined a lion's demeanor and capabilities; therefore, it was a fact in the Lion's coward mind. These research claims confirmed for Lion that he had failed his role.

After Scarecrow and Dorothy convinced Lion to seek courage from the Wizard, they all merrily continued the journey to Oz, skipping down the yellow brick road. They were all pumped up and very hopeful of reaching the Wizard.

Dorothy, always being the positive one, encouraged the others that they too could live their dream. They were *hoping* she was right. They traveled that yellow brick road on *Dorothy's* faith, not their own. This is okay. She held the light of truth for them.

With this light, they could see the possibilities. Faith and self-confidence was strengthened. Each step on the yellow brick road was made with absolute expectation that what they were seeking could indeed manifest.

We need each other in that respect, someone to hold the light for us or someone who can see the light for us, so we can stay on the path of our goal. Eventually, we will see the light for ourselves.

Lion was the incarnation of Zeke, the worker who courageously saved Dorothy when she fell into the pig sty on the Kansas farm. He was quite shaken as he pulled her out of that muddy sty. Love obliterated fear and uncovered courage. Courage manifested as an expression of love.

Zeke told Dorothy, "She [Miss Gulch] ain't nothin' to be afraid of; have a little courage, that's all."[14]

Wicked Witches

The Wicked Witches

"We do not need to give up our power to that which threatens us."
– Helen Gordon

W icked Witches
(secrets, what/whose out to get you)

Upon her arrival, Dorothy was celebrated for having killed the Wicked Witch of the East. Only the witch's black and white prison-stripped socks and red shoes were visible.

An invisible force representing secrets, is what we use to condemn and imprison ourselves. Those secrets are the roots to our guilt that the ego uses to devalue our existence, talents and worthiness.

Dorothy immediately apologized for having caused such a bad thing to happen in their land; however, the Munchkins saw nothing bad about it, they were overwhelmingly joyous about their new freedom.

Further along the journey, Dorothy, Scarecrow, Tin Man and Lion ran into the Wicked Witch of the West, alleged proof that there were powers to which they were weak and helpless.

How could they possibly reach their goal with something so powerfully evil against them, fiercely blocking the way to their destiny? We sometimes feel we have no way or power to reach our goals due to a block of some kind.

With greed, Wicked Witch wanted to control everyone and everything and was determined to get even more power by taking the ruby slippers from Dorothy. But we do not need to give up our power to that which threatens us, especially to something or someone so powerless.

At one point, Dorothy even tried to give the ruby slippers to Wicked Witch, but even the witch could not remove them from Dorothy's feet. We can deny our power, but it can never be given away.

Denying who we are cannot change who we are, which are powerful beings. We can deny the love of God, but we cannot be without it. Dorothy's shoes were divine protection and guidance to the love and home she thought was lost forever.

But how could they conquer this most evil and powerful thing (Wicked Witch) that blocked them from their desires?

It was a desperate gesture of love that worked. The witch set Scarecrow afire for entertainment; however, out of love, Dorothy spontaneously dashed a bucket of water on him to save his life.

The witch's intent was to amuse herself by harming Scarecrow with fire, what he feared most. Fire was deadly for him. Things looked pretty fatal for Scarecrow, but it was a blessing disguised as evil. Instead, the evil deed killed the witch. As the water was dashed upon Scarecrow to save his life, it also splashed on the witch. Water is what she feared most because it was deadly for her.

Water, the source of life, what seemed to be no weapon at all, was what ultimately killed the evil witch. This was a simple and readily available tool to end evil. Like most solutions, the method to end this evil always existed; the right method simply had not been applied until then.

What sometimes seems like bad luck, evil or harmful in our lives is merely a gift to place us closer to our goal. The evil intention does not happen. As believable as it appeared, their bondage in the witch's castle was never going to be permanent.

At the beginning of Dorothy's story, she saw Miss Gulch riding her bicycle in the tumultuous sky past the window of the spinning house. Right before her eyes, Miss Gulch morphed into the Wicked Witch of the West who later sought revenge against Dorothy for killing her sister.

Dorothy duplicated this alleged enemy, victimization and character in her beautiful imaginary world of Oz. In Kansas, Miss Gulch sought revenge against Dorothy for being a nuisance each day.

What We Desire

7

What We Desire

"We are all Dorothy and her friends. We have the, brains, love, courage and power to find our way home, to reach our goals, and to live our dreams." – Helen Gordon

D esire (it was always there)

Throughout this journey, Dorothy, Tin Man, Scarecrow, and Lion's determination was supported by the skills they already possessed. Brainless Scarecrow concocted clever ways to move beyond obstacles to rescue Dorothy from the Wicked Witch who had blocked their path to the Wizard. Heartless Tin Man worried and cried over Dorothy's well-being. Cowardly Lion accepted his charge to invade the witch's castle to save Dorothy's life. Dorothy provided purpose for them all to continue the journey.

Finally, they met the Wizard of Oz at Emerald City but were devastated when they found that he was fake. After such a long treacherous journey, they discovered that what they were seeking outside of themselves (Wizard) was no more powerful than they.

Wizard recognized the truth about them and proceeded to reveal their capabilities to them in a form they could proudly recognize and accept.

Scarecrow was given a diploma. It was merely a piece of paper acknowledging he had a brain. It did not require a transplant of a new brain. There was no void to fill; there was no lack of what he wanted to know.

That piece of paper was what convinced Scarecrow that he *finally had a brain.*

Upon acceptance of a scroll of printed intellectual confirmation (diploma), Scarecrow then blurted out the Pythagorean Theorem. That mathematical theorem was always in his head (brain). Faith in himself, strengthened by printed acknowledgment, just allowed his exceptional intelligence to come forth and express through him.

Next, Wizard pinned a large impressive medal of courage on Lion. That simple medal convinced Lion that he could do anything and fear nothing! He too had tangible proof acknowledging his tremendous courage.

Tin Man cried often throughout the journey, which rusted his joints. Yet it was not until the Wizard handed him a heart-shaped ticking clock that he was convinced he had a heart. For him, the clock ticked (beat) as a heart. Again, physical proof of the emotion that already existed within him.

Their desired abilities were always being demonstrated, but they had not noticed for hopelessly blaming, denying and focusing on what they could **not** do, so much so that they believed they could not. Their abilities had been concealed by self-pity and attitudes of defeat.

Each one of them always had what they were seeking: intellect, love and courage. All of these talents also existed in each of them; which one they chose to emphasize and value most was different.

Dorothy's turn came to get what she was seeking, to float home in the hot-air balloon with the Wizard. While retrieving Toto, she missed her take-off and believed that to be her last chance to get back home. Wizard did not know how to operate the balloon to return to pick her up. Devastated, she watched her dream drift away beyond her reach.

How often do we think we have missed our last chance at something, missed qualifying by a few points on an exam, missed a deadline, or miscalculated? Perhaps it seems the opportunity of a lifetime just slipped right through our fingers.

New opportunities will never cease to greet us. These are only thoughts of lack and limitation. There is no limit to the power of God and no last opportunity ever happens.

There is no one way of doing something, no one way to reach the goal. Yet we often limit our vision of how something should be achieved, never looking outside the box or stepping beyond the door to create another way to obtain it. Instead, we grieve over the seeming loss and stare hopelessly at our balloon (opportunity) adrift without us and ask, "Why me?"

Also, Dorothy's last minute frantic search for Toto and her emotional goodbyes of regret for leaving friends behind, represent hesitation to grasp opportunity she had worked very hard to get. Unconscious self-sabotage and fear of success create failure.

In the midst of Dorothy's moment of self-pity and seeming hopelessness, Tin Man aimlessly called out for help and a beautiful Good Witch appeared. The others asked the Good Witch why Dorothy did not get what she wanted; everyone else had their dreams fulfilled. The Good Witch answered, "It was not enough to want."[15]

When the Good Witch asked Dorothy what she had learned from this long journey, Dorothy paused and then replied, "If I ever go looking for my heart's desire again, I won't go looking any further than my own backyard [within me]. Because if it isn't there, I never really lost it to begin with." [16]

All we need is within us. Right where we are is the answer. We are always at home.

The others asked why she was sent to the Wizard when that was all she had to know. The Good Witch responded, "She wouldn't have believed me. She had to learn it [do the work] for herself."[17]

It is good practice to sometimes take pause and reflect on our life's opportunities. As with Dorothy, we may hesitate at the opportunities that lead us to our goals for fear of leaving something or someone we value behind, or feel we need to give up (sacrifice) something.

We refer to those things as sacrifices we are not willing to make. Dorothy did not need to sacrifice anything real to board the balloon. She only had to relinquish her valuables in form and fantasy in exchange for reality, which had everything she wanted.

Yes, it may be difficult to ignore the seeming danger when the witch is scowling in our faces; however, the witch (ego) deliberately does this because she knows that the bigger the fear, the weaker the person and the easier it is to control them.

To remain conscious of our power, we must control the fear. Controlling fear helps us make decisions for intelligent planning.

Additionally, controlling anger makes for executing the plan successfully. We can navigate through this world, achieve whatever we desire or go home.

We are all Dorothy and her friends. We have the brains, courage, love and power to find our way home, to reach our goals, and to live our dreams.

As the Course says, we are merely trying to find our way back home to heaven. Use the yellow brick road (inner guidance) to find it. Consciously, keep wearing those ruby slippers. Trust each step.

The Wizard

The Wizard

"We want the magic and the impossible to be done for us without our participation." – Helen Gordon

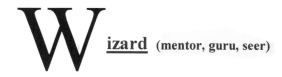

Wizard (mentor, guru, seer)

The Wizard in our lives sees the Truth about us, our abilities and gifts. As a sought after mentor (seer, guru), he brings those invisible traits forth into the physical that we may believe the Truth about ourselves.

We want the magic and the impossible to be performed for us even without our participation. Surely the Wizard could do it.

But the Wizard was no more powerful than Dorothy or her friends.

Wizard provided a physical confirmation of the talents and gifts each one already possessed. They had been using those abilities throughout the journey but did not recognize it.

Their focus on their inabilities obliterated recognition that what they needed was within them throughout the entire journey. Although they did not each wear a pair of red slippers to remind them of their power, it was always within them.

Our personal wizards merely help reveal to us what we already know to be true. They serve to reveal the intellect, love courage and power that are always within us.

A personal Wizard can support us through prayer, with direct assistance, and by keeping sight of the truth about our divinity. Who we are is complete. What we do is perfectly guided. What we become as a result is our gift to the World.

The Balloon

9

The Balloon

"New opportunities will never cease to greet us. These are only thoughts of lack and limitation. There is no limit to the power of God and no last opportunity ever happens."

– Helen Gordon

Balloon (Opportunity)

The balloon was designated as Dorothy's means of getting back home, her only desire and reason for her journey to Emerald City. Although that **form** of opportunity may not come again, opportunity will appear again in some form, faster than we think.

Dorothy supported and encouraged the others to the very end. It was a sense of helping others as a means of meeting the requirements to receive her own desires.

Sometimes we are convinced that what we need to do for ourselves can wait, taking less priority than other's needs and goals. After all, we cannot be selfish and expect to receive.

The balloon left without Dorothy which she interpreted as her last chance to receive what she so strongly desired. This is lack and limitation thinking. Dorothy did not miss the opportunity, she passed it up. She did not take action; however, she would rally that she did.

There was a story to support how earnestly she had taken action. On her treacherous journey along the yellow brick road from Munchkin Land to Emerald City, she encountered hunger, a lion, nearly death in the poppy field, an evil witch, abuse and imprisonment. All this she survived, determined to exchange fantasy for reality. She weathered the whole journey until the exchange for reality was right before her.

It is our thoughts and beliefs that make the goal seem impossible or difficult to reach. We must always take the last step of the journey toward that goal to complete it.

The long goodbyes were a form of delay, self-sabotage and difficulty in receiving. The thing she so badly wanted was right there in her reach, yet she did not hold on to it firmly. The ego disguised it as emotional goodbyes to wonderful friends.

The love of whatever seems left behind will always be with us regardless of the distance travelled because love is eternal and boundless. It is everywhere all the time.

We must board the balloon at our depot of life. It has other scheduled stops to make to fulfill other dreams. It does not make others wait until we awaken.

Awakening

10

The Awakening

"Strength Dorothy did not know she had, led her to the Wizard and eventually back home."

– *Helen Gordon*

W**aking up** (seeing Truth)

Dorothy woke up from her injury, grateful to find that she was at home--in her bed, surrounded by love, friends and family, not enemies. It all seemed so real, yet it had all been a dream of a journey to Oz.

In that moment of awakening, Dorothy realized that each person at that Kansas farm had played a role in her dream, disguised as a different character [past life]. Only their form had changed. All of them had always loved her and wanted the best for her. With her awakening, she recognized their love for her. She could appreciate them just the way they were, each with their own needs, shortcomings, and ways of living life.

Dorothy did not need to diminish the experiences she had while on that journey. She lived it to find her way back home to understand reality. Strength Dorothy did not know she had, led her to the Wizard and eventually back home.

The journey had been an empowering illusion, happening only in her mind, with lessons for inner growth, forgiveness and gratitude. It all seemed so real and at times things seemed threatening, unfair, or hopeless. In the dream, she had lost everything but Toto, and regretfully had to face the witches of a new world.

Those negative things only existed in her created fantasy world of Oz because she had never left home but in her mind. Although the danger (witch) and other characters were not real in Oz, it did not diminish reality even when she responded as if they did.

Each character symbolized what we will or are going through in our human experience, as we seek our own Wizard, meet many witches, and journey to our own created land of Oz. The road may not be yellow or even brick. We may journey on a dirt path, by ship, by airplane, by train, etc.

Whatever the form of travel for our life's journey, it will be real for us. No form of the journey is bad, just different, as we find our way back home. Enjoy the trip.

Symbolism

11

Symbolism

"What we go through or will go through is harmless and always under our control." – Helen Gordon

Symbols (conscious perception)

Apples

Coercion. Manipulation.

Aunt Em

She was a worrier, straight-laced, hard worker and serious about life. Did not take the time to play. Unbalanced life.

Basket

Treasures. What is important to us.

Backyard

Inner intelligence. Within yourself. Right where you are is the answer you seek. You must do the work from your own backyard.

Castle Door at Oz

What you think is between you and the final manifestation of your dream. What you can overcome.

Emerald City

Achievement. Success at reaching a goal. With a great deal of hard work, achieving a goal such as a job promotion, relationship, financial status, etc., only to find disappointment once you are there. The grass is greener on the other side attitude.

Success does not look or feel the way you envisioned. It is still not enough.

Eye of the Tornado
Turmoil of life. Confused and overwhelmed by life. Consumed by fear of things around you.

Farm
Simplicity of life. Provides.

Flying Monkeys
Imagined enemies or ill fate lurking in wait to get you at any time.

Good Witches
Teacher. Wisdom. Mentor. Caring. There are people in your life who share their wisdom with you to help you succeed. Glinda helped Dorothy get started and helped her to make the last step but did not do it for her.

Miss Elvira Gulch

Structure. Fighter for ones rights. Closed-minded, lacks patience, very judgmental, resentful and condemning. Stays in the box.

Hour Glass

Pressure and anxiety of time. Running out of time.

Marvel the Magician

Guilt. White lie. Deceit.

Munchkin

Dependence. Independence. Sometimes there are people in your life who depend upon you to a point of exhaustion (financially and emotionally).

Every time you start a task, somehow you end up helping someone else with his or hers? You are convinced that what you need to do for yourself can wait, taking less priority than other's needs and goals.

Oil Can

Provides the freedom to move about easier and to express yourself. Things are within your reach.

Oz

A physical place or method of escape and comfort. Beach, church, meditation, alcohol, drugs, food, retreat, seminar, etc.

Pig Sty

A fun experience that turns frightening. You emerge unscathed. Something you should not repeat again.

Poppies (Flowers)

Mental escape through intoxication from something that appears harmless and inviting.

Dorothy succumbs to its affect. You have those who try to pull you out of it (rehabilitation) as Dorothy's companions did. One joined her and the other two remained strong, always conscious of the harm it was bringing to their friends. They knew how deadly it could be.

Rain
Rehabilitation.

Ruby Red Slippers
The power within you.

Scarecrow
Intellectually challenged or embarrassed. Hung up on some negative belief about himself. Self-conscious. Low self-esteem.

Salon/Spa at Oz
Preparation to receive your desires.

Smoke of the Wizard's Apparition

Lies. Deceit. Superficial.

Striped Socks of the first Wicked Witch

Imprisonment of something divine. Fatality of the misuse of power.

Tin Man

Procrastinates, feels paralyzed, and makes no progress or effort. Numb and out of shape. Have you ever found yourself paralyzed in life? There is so much to do and you want to do, but you cannot seem to get going?

Tornado

Life feels out of control. Chaos. It appears you have no control over what is going on around you. Life seems to be getting darker.

Toto

Loving, promiscuous, and inconsiderate. Just out to have fun.

Water

Can save or take a life. Dual purpose. An evil intent that serves as a holy encounter.

Wicked Witches

Vindication and greed. Temper, jealousy, envy, power struggle, obsession with control.

Wind

Anger. Creates chaos, turmoil and disconnect.

Wizard

Someone offering something you have been convinced as having great value that you must have in order to live a happier life. A guru and problem solver. That someone whom you think knows more than you do.

Yellow Brick Road

Guidance of your inner Spirit, that holy part of you. It is readily available to guide you in your journey called life when you listen to it. Divine inner Voice. Intuition.

Journey Home

12

The Journey Home

"Peace of mind will escape us until we open to change. In change is the gift of peace, power and piety. What we become is larger than our expectations; what we gain is beyond our expectations; what we learn is beyond what we thought we were intellectually capable."

–Helen Gordon

T<u>he Journey Home</u> (going within)

It is time to take action. Until you have run the course, you can never win the race. It takes more than just reading about how to do it.

Answers to these questions will help you identify people you have interacted with as you traveled along your yellow brick road of life.

As you do this, it should become clearer as to the role each one has played in your life to support your success or to help you become stronger. Each one has taught you something and prepared you in some way to achieve what you desire.

By now you have recognized the shortcomings and strengths of each Oz character within you in some form that exists now or in the past.

Note the shortcomings as things to release and the strengths as things to build upon as you move through the questions on the following pages. Space is provided to answer the questions directly in the book or you can use a separate piece of paper.

Repeat the questions again in six months because these characters will return in your life to support you through the next phase. Reading this book again at that time will be a plus. The additional clarity will help anchor the understanding stronger and deeper.

1. Name your wicked witch (three or less, male and/or female).

1.

2.

3.

What do they have in common (if more than one wicked witch)?

_____

_____

_____

_____

_____

2. What did you learn from the relationship(s)?

Anything, even if it seems irrelevant to this book's teachings.

_____

_____

_____

_____

_____

_____

_____

_____

_____

_____

_____

3. List the good about the relationship(s).

Although you may find it difficult, look for even the smallest good.

_____

_____

_____

_____

_____

_____

_____

_____

_____

_____

_____

4. Name your Good Witch (four or less).

1.

2.

3.

4.

5. List their similar traits and contributions to your sanity.

Those listed in question #4.

_____

_____

_____

_____

_____

_____

_____

.
_____

_____

_____

_____

_____

_____

6. Who has been heavily dependent upon you for their success or happiness? (name three)

If there is no one, list whom you have depended upon for success and happiness.

1.

2.

3.

7. Have you sacrificed your own success for theirs (or vice versa)? If so, how?

_____

_____

_____

_____

_____

_____

_____

_____

_____

_____

_____

_____

_____

8. List the traits, habits or thoughts of Dorothy that you also see in you.

_____

_____

_____

_____

_____

_____

_____

_____

_____

_____

_____

_____

9. What love or thing do you fear losing?

_____

_____

_____

_____

_____

_____

_____

_____

_____

_____

_____

_____

_____

_____

10. Name at least one trait, habit or situation you have that is similar to each character or place in the story.

Review their meaning in the previous chapter on symbolism, to help you decide.

a. Wicked Witch of the East

b. Wicked Witch of the West

c. Good witch

d. Munchkin

e. Scarecrow

f. Tin Man

g. Lion

h. Wizard

i. Toto

j. Aunt Em

k. Miss Gulch

l. Marvel the Magician

m. Land of Oz

n. Emerald City

11. Name at least one thing in your life that is represented by the following symbols.

Review their meaning in the previous chapter on symbolism, to help you decide.

a. Apples

b. Backyard

c. Castle Door at Oz

d. Poppies

e. Flying Monkeys

f. Hour Glass

g. Farm

h. Pig Sty

i. Rain

j. Striped socks of the first
    Wicked Witch

k. Smoke of the Wizard's
    Apparition

l. Salon/Spa

m. Tornado

12. What has been your experience with:

Review their meaning in the previous chapter on symbolism, to help you decide.

a. Yellow Brick Road

b. Ruby Red Slippers

c. Castle Door at Oz

Footnotes

[1] Wizard of Oz, 1939 MGM movie.
[2] Ibid
[3] Ibid
[4] Ibid
[5] Ibid
[6] Ibid
[7] Ibid
[8] Ibid
[9] Ibid
[10] Ibid
[11] Ibid
[12] Ibid
[13] Ibid
[14] Ibid
[15] Ibid
[16] Ibid
[17] Ibid

Made in the USA
Charleston, SC
21 September 2012